GPT-4o
Predicted Outputs and Why It's Faster Than Ever Before

How OpenAI Is Reshaping Workflows,
From Coding to Content Creation

J. Andy Peters

Table of Contents

Introduction

GPT-4o represents a remarkable leap in the evolution of artificial intelligence, building upon the foundation of its predecessors while introducing features that redefine efficiency and practicality. This advanced model is not just a tool for generating text but a sophisticated system designed to understand, adapt, and optimize processes in ways that align with the ever-growing demands of modern technology. Its ability to deliver nuanced responses, handle complex queries, and integrate seamlessly into a variety of workflows makes it an indispensable resource for developers, content creators, and professionals across industries.

One of the standout innovations introduced with GPT-4o is the "Predicted Outputs" feature, a groundbreaking capability that addresses a common challenge in AI interactions: speed. Traditionally, AI models generate responses token by token, a process that can be time-consuming, especially when dealing with large datasets, extensive codebases, or lengthy documents. Predicted Outputs changes the game by allowing users to provide hints or partial responses that the model can build upon, significantly reducing the time required for processing and delivering results. This feature is particularly beneficial for tasks where much of the input remains constant, enabling the AI to focus on what truly needs to change rather than starting from scratch each time.

In today's fast-paced, tech-driven world, the demand for speed and accuracy has never been greater. From coding and data analysis to content creation and project management, the ability to complete tasks quickly without sacrificing quality is a competitive advantage. GPT-4o, with its Predicted Outputs feature, steps in as a solution to this need, offering not just faster responses but smarter, more targeted ones. It empowers professionals to streamline repetitive tasks, optimize workflows, and focus on innovation rather than routine operations. By embracing this capability, users are poised to unlock new levels of productivity and redefine what's possible with AI in the digital age.

Chapter 1: The Evolution of GPT Models

The evolution from GPT-3 to GPT-4o reflects a significant progression in the capabilities and practical applications of artificial intelligence. GPT-3, celebrated for its vast knowledge and fluency, set the stage as a versatile model capable of generating human-like text across countless domains. Its ability to understand context and produce coherent, nuanced responses made it a pivotal tool for developers, researchers, and creators alike. However, as the demands on AI systems grew, so too did the expectations for speed, efficiency, and adaptability—leading to the development of GPT-4o.

One of the key advancements in this journey was the refinement of contextual understanding. While GPT-3 was impressive in its ability to handle broad topics, GPT-4o introduced a more nuanced comprehension of intricate tasks, enabling it to perform more precisely in specialized applications. This leap was driven by enhancements in its training architecture, which allowed the model to process and prioritize information with greater accuracy. It became better equipped to handle complex queries, adapt to user-specific requirements, and deliver results tailored to highly specific contexts.

Another milestone was the integration of features designed to improve efficiency, such as "Predicted Outputs." This innovation marked a shift in how AI generates responses by allowing users to provide partial predictions, effectively speeding up tasks that previously required step-by-step token generation. The feature reflects a broader trend in AI development: moving beyond raw computational power toward intelligent optimizations that make interactions faster and more intuitive.

Equally important was the expansion of the model's application capabilities. GPT-4o not only builds on the general-purpose strengths of GPT-3 but also introduces optimizations for coding, content editing, and data manipulation. Developers, for instance, can now perform iterative code adjustments or large-scale document edits with unprecedented efficiency. These advancements cater to the growing demand for tools that not only perform well but also integrate seamlessly into existing workflows.

The journey from GPT-3 to GPT-4o is a testament to how AI models continue to evolve in response to real-world needs. With each iteration, the focus shifts from proving what's possible to enhancing usability, speed, and accuracy. GPT-4o embodies this evolution, offering not just a more powerful AI system but one designed with practical, everyday applications in mind—meeting the rising expectations of users across industries.

GPT-4o stands apart from its predecessors by introducing a suite of innovations aimed at enhancing both speed and precision. While earlier models like GPT-3 were celebrated for their ability to generate human-like responses, GPT-4o builds on this foundation with targeted optimizations that address key challenges in workflow efficiency. The advancements in GPT-4o are not just incremental; they represent a deliberate shift toward making AI more adaptable, intuitive, and practical for real-world applications.

One of the defining differences lies in its approach to processing information. GPT-4o incorporates smarter token management systems, allowing it to handle larger and more complex datasets with remarkable efficiency. This improvement is especially evident in tasks that involve iterative changes or partial updates, where GPT-4o excels by focusing on the specific areas that require modification. Instead of reprocessing entire inputs, it intelligently narrows its scope, ensuring faster and more precise outputs.

The integration of the "Predicted Outputs" feature is where GPT-4o truly sets a new benchmark. This breakthrough stems from the recognition that many tasks, particularly in coding, content editing, and data manipulation, involve repetitive elements. By allowing users to provide partial predictions or templates, GPT-4o can leapfrog redundant computations, delivering results in a fraction of the time. This feature not only boosts speed but also reduces cognitive load on users, making AI interactions smoother and more intuitive.

Another area of distinction is the model's adaptability. While earlier iterations were highly capable of generating original content, GPT-4o introduces a more refined ability to work within constraints, whether it's adjusting lines of code, refining text, or streamlining datasets. This adaptability makes it a preferred tool for developers and professionals who need to make precise changes without disrupting the broader structure of their work.

The "Predicted Outputs" feature, in particular, signals a shift in how AI systems are designed to interact with users. Rather than simply responding to open-ended queries, GPT-4o empowers users to guide the AI by offering a framework or prediction.

This collaborative approach bridges the gap between human intent and machine execution, setting a new standard for efficiency. Tasks that previously required multiple iterations can now be completed seamlessly in one step, showcasing the transformative potential of this innovation.

By addressing the limitations of its predecessors and introducing forward-thinking features like "Predicted Outputs," GPT-4o positions itself as a model designed for the future. It not only enhances what AI can do but also redefines how users interact with it—making workflows faster, smarter, and more aligned with the demands of an increasingly tech-driven world.

Chapter 2: What Are Predicted Outputs?

The "Predicted Outputs" feature in GPT-4o is a transformative innovation that redefines how AI models generate responses. At its core, this feature allows users to provide a prediction or partial framework of what the output should include, enabling the AI to build upon the provided information rather than generating everything from scratch. This targeted approach significantly accelerates the response time, particularly for tasks involving repetitive or partially known outputs.

Traditionally, AI models generate responses token by token—where each token represents a word, part of a word, or even a piece of code. This sequential process, while effective, can be time-consuming when dealing with lengthy or complex tasks. For instance, if you were editing a large codebase or document, the AI would process every token in the response, even those unchanged from the input, leading to inefficiencies and longer waiting times.

"Predicted Outputs" disrupts this traditional method by introducing a more streamlined workflow. Instead of starting from a blank slate, the user provides the model with a partial response or prediction. This could be an existing piece of code, a section of a document, or a baseline structure for the output. The model then evaluates this input, identifies areas where changes are needed, and focuses exclusively on generating the new tokens required to complete the task. Unchanged portions of the prediction are accepted as-is, skipping the need for reprocessing and drastically reducing the time spent generating a response.

For example, imagine you are working on a piece of code where only a single line needs to be updated. With traditional token generation, the model would analyze and rewrite the entire block of code, even if most of it remains unaltered. In contrast, "Predicted Outputs" lets you provide the existing code as a baseline, allowing the AI to adjust only the necessary portions. The result is faster output with minimal redundancy.

This feature is particularly advantageous in scenarios where tasks are repetitive or predictable. In these cases, the model doesn't waste resources on regenerating unchanged elements, allowing users to complete their work more efficiently. By focusing only on the areas requiring modification, "Predicted Outputs" ensures that the AI delivers results that are not only faster but also more aligned with user expectations.

In summary, "Predicted Outputs" shifts the paradigm from exhaustive token-by-token generation to a collaborative process where users guide the AI. By combining predictive input with targeted adjustments, this feature sets a new standard for efficiency, making it a cornerstone of GPT-4o's capabilities and a key differentiator from traditional AI workflows.

Predictions play a pivotal role in streamlining responses by providing a foundation for the AI to work from, cutting down on unnecessary processing and improving both speed and efficiency. By offering a partial output or anticipated structure, users allow the model to focus solely on what needs to be modified or generated, rather than starting from a blank slate. This shift not only saves time but also creates a more seamless interaction, especially for tasks with repetitive or partially known elements.

When predictions are provided, the AI uses them as a reference to assess what matches and what needs adjustment. This process ensures that unchanged portions are processed quickly, while only new or differing elements are generated. For example, in coding tasks, you might provide an existing block of code with instructions to modify specific lines. The AI recognizes the consistent parts of the input, bypasses their regeneration, and concentrates on implementing the changes requested. The result is a highly targeted output that aligns precisely with user expectations.

This approach also minimizes redundancy. In traditional workflows, the model would evaluate and regenerate the entire response, even if much of it remained the same. With predictions, the model effectively "locks in" the parts of the response that don't need alteration, streamlining the process and reducing the computational load. This targeted focus not only accelerates response times but also improves the overall efficiency of interactions.

Another advantage of using predictions is the ability to handle complex tasks incrementally. In situations where users are working on iterative updates—such as refining code, tweaking text, or making small adjustments to data—predictions allow the model to adapt dynamically without rehashing unchanged elements. This capability is especially beneficial for large-scale tasks, where reprocessing everything from scratch would be both time-consuming and resource-intensive.

Furthermore, predictions enhance the accuracy of the output. By providing a clear framework or starting point, users help guide the AI's response, reducing the likelihood of errors or misinterpretations. For instance, when updating a document, you can specify the unchanged portions and highlight the sections requiring edits. The AI then tailors its response to those exact requirements, ensuring a more precise and relevant result.

The efficiency gains from predictions extend to a variety of practical applications, from coding and document editing to data manipulation. Whether you're refactoring a codebase, revising a blog post, or updating a dataset, predictions allow the AI to focus its energy where it's needed most. This focus results in faster responses, fewer errors, and a smoother workflow, making "Predicted Outputs" a game-changing feature for GPT-4o users.

Ultimately, the ability to streamline responses through predictions underscores the collaborative potential of AI. By enabling users to guide the process with context and intent, GPT-4o achieves a level of efficiency and precision that transforms how we approach repetitive and detail-oriented tasks. This innovation not only saves time but also empowers users to work smarter, ensuring that every interaction with the model is optimized for success.

Chapter 3: The Speed Revolution

"Predicted Outputs" introduces a dramatic shift in efficiency, making it a cornerstone of GPT-4o's innovation. By leveraging user-provided predictions, the model bypasses unnecessary processing, enabling faster task completion while maintaining accuracy and quality. This feature has led to measurable improvements in various workflows, with some tasks being completed in a fraction of the time they once required.

One of the most notable examples comes from coding tasks. Before "Predicted Outputs," editing a large code file required the model to evaluate and regenerate the entire response, often taking as long as 70 seconds for complex files. With this new feature, the AI focuses solely on the sections needing updates, reducing the processing time to just 20 seconds—a speed improvement of over 70%. This efficiency stems from the model's ability to skip generating unchanged portions of the code, concentrating only on new or modified elements.

In the world of coding, this time-saving capability proves invaluable. For instance, a developer refactoring a TypeScript class might need to update a single property, such as changing `username` to `email`. By providing the existing code as a prediction, the AI quickly identifies the consistent parts and modifies only the relevant section, completing the task in seconds. Similarly, when adding a new route to a JavaScript server setup, the model incorporates the new code seamlessly into the existing structure without reprocessing the rest of the file. These focused updates allow developers to iterate more rapidly, freeing up time for more strategic problem-solving.

Content creation is another area where "Predicted Outputs" excels. Imagine a writer updating a blog post where most of the content remains unchanged. By supplying the stable portions of the article as a prediction, the AI zeroes in on the specific edits requested—such as rephrasing a paragraph or adding new information—without reanalyzing the entire text. This precision not only speeds up the process but also ensures stylistic consistency, which is crucial for maintaining a coherent voice across multiple revisions.

Data manipulation tasks also benefit significantly from this feature. Consider a scenario where an analyst is working on a large dataset with only a few entries requiring modification. Instead of reprocessing the entire dataset, the AI focuses solely on the specified updates. This capability is particularly valuable when working with massive data files, where time savings can translate into greater productivity and reduced computational costs.

The efficiency gains from "Predicted Outputs" are not just theoretical; they have practical implications across industries. Whether it's a developer debugging code, a writer polishing content, or a data scientist refining datasets, this feature accelerates workflows while preserving quality. By reducing redundant computations and focusing on precise changes, GPT-4o empowers users to work smarter, saving time and resources while achieving better outcomes. This evolution in AI capabilities represents a turning point, setting new benchmarks for speed, efficiency, and practicality in everyday applications.

Streaming mode in GPT-4o enhances real-time AI processing by delivering responses incrementally, providing users with immediate results as the model generates each part of the output. This approach is a significant improvement over traditional methods, where the AI processes the entire response before presenting it to the user. Streaming mode minimizes delays, making workflows more efficient and interactive.

The fundamental advantage of streaming lies in its ability to deliver results in chunks. As the AI processes the user's input, it begins sending portions of the output right away, rather than waiting until the entire response is complete. This not only reduces the perceived wait time but also allows users to interact with the response as it's being generated. For instance, a developer refining code can start reviewing and implementing changes immediately, even before the entire output is finalized. Similarly, a content creator can edit and approve sections of text in real time, speeding up the revision process.

Streaming mode pairs seamlessly with the "Predicted Outputs" feature, amplifying its efficiency. When users provide predictions, the AI quickly processes the accepted tokens and begins generating new or modified sections. This real-time feedback loop ensures that users see the results almost instantly, allowing for faster iterations and more dynamic interactions. The ability to adjust and refine predictions as the output unfolds further streamlines the workflow, enabling a more collaborative and intuitive experience.

Consider a scenario where a data scientist is working with a large dataset. Instead of waiting for the AI to process the entire file, streaming mode allows the analyst to receive and review updates incrementally. This incremental delivery enables quicker validation of changes, reducing the overall time required to complete the task. In coding, streaming mode is equally transformative. A developer adding new functionality to a script can see the updated segments in real time, implementing changes faster and catching potential errors sooner.

Another key benefit of streaming is its adaptability to diverse tasks and environments. Whether you're working on a simple blog update or tackling complex coding challenges, the ability to receive immediate feedback ensures that the AI adapts fluidly to your needs. It transforms static interactions into dynamic exchanges, where users can actively engage with the AI's output as it evolves.

By combining real-time processing with the targeted efficiency of "Predicted Outputs," streaming mode represents a significant leap in AI responsiveness. It not only saves time but also enhances the overall user experience, making workflows more intuitive and productive. This capability underscores GPT-4o's commitment to aligning AI technology with the practical needs of users, delivering results that are faster, smarter, and more seamlessly integrated into everyday tasks.

Chapter 4: How Predicted Outputs Work

The mechanics of "Predicted Outputs" revolve around enabling users to guide GPT-4o with partial predictions, streamlining the model's response generation by focusing on what needs to change while skipping over what remains constant. This process involves two key components: feeding partial predictions and the token acceptance and rejection mechanism.

Feeding partial predictions to the model begins with the user providing a segment of the expected output. This prediction serves as a framework for the AI, helping it understand what parts of the response are already correct and where adjustments or new content are required. For example, in coding, you might input an existing class structure with a note to change specific properties. Similarly, in content creation, you might provide an article draft with only the sections needing updates flagged for modification. This input acts as a blueprint, guiding the AI toward the desired result without starting from scratch.

Once the prediction is provided, GPT-4o processes it through a token acceptance and rejection system. Tokens are the building blocks of the AI's output, representing words, parts of words, or pieces of code. The model evaluates the provided tokens against the task requirements, determining which parts of the prediction align with the output it would generate. Tokens that match the prediction are accepted and integrated into the response without further processing. This bypass not only saves time but also ensures that the unchanged portions of the input remain consistent with the user's intent.

Tokens that deviate from the AI's intended output are flagged for rejection. These rejected tokens are discarded, and the model generates replacements to address the discrepancies. For instance, if a prediction includes a property in a code snippet that no longer matches the updated structure, the

AI identifies and corrects it. However, it's important to note that while rejected tokens are discarded, the computational cost of processing them is still incurred. This means that providing accurate predictions not only speeds up the task but also minimizes unnecessary token processing, optimizing both time and cost.

This token management system allows the model to work more efficiently, honing in on the areas that require attention while preserving the integrity of the unchanged elements. For users, this translates into a faster, more reliable workflow. Tasks like refactoring code, revising documents, or editing datasets are completed with precision, as the AI seamlessly integrates the accepted tokens and focuses its computational power on the rejected ones.

The acceptance and rejection process is a critical aspect of how "Predicted Outputs" operates, making it possible for GPT-4o to handle complex tasks with remarkable speed and accuracy. By leveraging partial predictions, users can guide the AI more effectively, ensuring that every interaction is optimized for their specific needs. This combination of targeted input and intelligent token processing highlights the sophistication of GPT-4o, offering a glimpse into the future of collaborative AI systems.

"Predicted Outputs" in GPT-4o is particularly transformative in scenarios where repetitive or structured tasks dominate, such as updating codebases or making incremental changes to scripts. Practical applications of this feature demonstrate how leveraging accurate predictions can dramatically improve efficiency and streamline workflows.

One clear example is updating a TypeScript class. Imagine you have a class named `User` that includes a property called `username`. You need to refactor the code so the property becomes `email` instead. Without "Predicted Outputs," the AI would process the entire block of code, generating each line from scratch, even those that don't require changes. With predictions, however, you can input the existing code as the framework. The AI recognizes the unchanged parts, skips reprocessing them, and modifies only the specified property. This targeted approach ensures the task is completed quickly and accurately, reducing redundant operations while maintaining the overall structure of the code.

Another practical use case involves adding routes to a server setup in JavaScript. Let's say you're working with a lightweight library like Hano to define server routes. The majority of your server structure is already in place, but you want to add a new route that responds with `Hello World`. By supplying the existing server code as a prediction, the AI focuses solely on integrating the new route. It doesn't reanalyze or rewrite the existing structure, instead directly appending the necessary line. This not only saves time but also preserves the integrity of your original setup, making the process more seamless and efficient.

The success of these examples hinges on the accuracy of the predictions provided. When users supply a clear and precise baseline, the model can lock onto the relevant elements, minimizing errors and ensuring that only the necessary changes are made. Accurate predictions help the AI to "understand" the scope of the task, allowing it to concentrate its computational efforts where they're needed most. For example, if your TypeScript class prediction correctly reflects the unchanged parts of the code, the AI only has to address the specific property update, avoiding unnecessary revisions.

This efficiency becomes even more pronounced in larger, more complex projects. For instance, in a project involving thousands of lines of code, the ability to supply partial predictions means the AI can focus exclusively on the sections requiring updates, leaving the rest untouched. This precision reduces processing time and prevents unintended changes, which is crucial for maintaining the stability of the overall codebase.

Ultimately, "Predicted Outputs" transforms tasks like updating TypeScript classes or adding JavaScript routes into streamlined, intuitive processes. By harnessing accurate predictions, developers can save significant time and effort, allowing them to focus on higher-level challenges and innovations. This capability illustrates the power of GPT-4o to not only improve productivity but also align AI's strengths with the practical needs of users across industries.

Chapter 5: Ideal Use Cases for Predicted Outputs

"Predicted Outputs" is particularly effective for handling repetitive and predictable tasks, where much of the input remains constant, and only specific elements need adjustment. By allowing users to provide partial predictions, GPT-4o focuses its efforts on the areas requiring change, delivering faster and more precise results. This feature proves invaluable in tasks such as code refactoring, blog post updates, and dataset modifications.

In **code refactoring**, developers often need to make small but crucial changes to existing codebases while maintaining the overall structure. For instance, updating a TypeScript class to rename a property or adjust a function's parameters typically involves scanning and modifying specific lines of code. With traditional AI workflows, the entire block of code might be regenerated, potentially introducing unnecessary changes. "Predicted Outputs" solves this by enabling developers to input the current code as a baseline. The AI evaluates this input, identifies the sections needing adjustment, and modifies only those parts, leaving the rest untouched. This targeted approach not only saves time but also ensures the stability and integrity of the codebase, making repetitive tasks like these significantly more efficient.

Blog post updates present another excellent application. Content creators frequently revisit older posts to add new information, refine existing sections, or adjust language to align with current trends. Instead of asking the AI to rewrite the entire article, creators can supply the unchanged portions as predictions, highlighting the areas that need updating. For example, if a blog post about a software update requires a new section on features introduced in the latest version, the AI can seamlessly integrate this addition while preserving the tone and structure of the original content. This ensures stylistic consistency and reduces the workload for creators, allowing them to manage updates across multiple posts with greater ease.

In **dataset modifications**, analysts often work with large collections of data where only a subset requires alteration. For example, updating entries in a customer database to reflect changes in contact details or correcting formatting errors involves repetitive adjustments to specific fields. By providing the stable portions of the dataset as a prediction, the AI processes only the sections needing modification. This capability is particularly valuable when working with large-scale datasets, where manually identifying and updating individual entries would be labor-intensive and error-prone. "Predicted Outputs" streamlines the process, ensuring that the updates are accurate and consistent across the dataset.

Across all these tasks, the repetitive and predictable nature of the work amplifies the benefits of "Predicted Outputs." By reducing redundancy and focusing on targeted changes, GPT-4o allows users to accomplish more in less time, while maintaining a high standard of quality. This efficiency is a game-changer for developers, writers, and analysts, freeing them from the tedium of repetitive tasks and enabling them to focus on more strategic and creative endeavors. In each case, the combination of speed, precision, and ease of use underscores the transformative potential of GPT-4o's predictive capabilities.

While "Predicted Outputs" excels in repetitive and predictable tasks, it is not designed for generating unique or entirely original content. This limitation stems from the feature's reliance on user-provided predictions as a baseline. For tasks requiring novel responses or content with no predictable patterns, "Predicted Outputs" lacks the flexibility to construct entirely new frameworks. In such cases, the AI's strength lies in traditional token-by-token generation, where it can explore possibilities without being constrained by a pre-existing structure.

When tasked with creating unique content, such as writing a story, crafting an original article, or designing a new algorithm from scratch, there's no baseline for the AI to anchor its predictions. The absence of patterns or repetitive elements makes "Predicted Outputs" ineffective. For instance, a blank canvas task like drafting a blog post about an emerging technology demands open-ended creativity. Here, the AI needs to generate everything from the ground up, an approach better suited to traditional workflows without prediction-based shortcuts.

However, where "Predicted Outputs" does shine is in programming, particularly for languages like Python, JavaScript, Go, and C++. Its performance across these languages highlights its ability to streamline coding tasks, though nuances in each language affect how efficiently the feature can be applied.

In **Python**, a language known for its readability and simplicity, "Predicted Outputs" handles refactoring and script updates with precision. Tasks like modifying functions, updating variable names, or adding new features to an existing module benefit greatly from the feature's ability to integrate changes without regenerating the entire code. Python's predictable syntax and widespread use in scripting and data science make it a prime candidate for leveraging predictions.

For **JavaScript**, especially in web development, "Predicted Outputs" simplifies iterative updates to frameworks, server setups, or front-end components. Adding new routes to servers, modifying API calls, or tweaking front-end logic can be completed in seconds, as the feature seamlessly incorporates changes into an existing codebase. JavaScript's versatility in both client- and server-side applications makes it a strong match for prediction-driven workflows.

In **Go**, a language popular for its efficiency and performance in building scalable systems, "Predicted Outputs" proves useful in refactoring or enhancing code while maintaining the robustness of Go's structured programming paradigm. Updates to structs, methods, or error-handling routines can be handled with precision, ensuring stability in performance-critical environments.

For **C++**, where complexity and performance optimization are paramount, "Predicted Outputs" supports tasks like modifying class definitions, updating function implementations, or integrating new modules into large projects. The feature ensures that consistent portions of the code remain intact, reducing the risk of unintended side effects in a language where precision is critical.

Comparing performance across these languages, the utility of "Predicted Outputs" becomes clear: it thrives where syntax and structure are predictable. Python and JavaScript, with their dynamic and modular nature, allow for more frequent updates and iterative changes, making the feature particularly effective. Go and C++, while more rigid, benefit from the feature's ability to handle targeted modifications without compromising overall integrity.

In summary, "Predicted Outputs" is a tool designed for optimization rather than invention. It excels in environments where patterns and predictability dominate, but it is not a substitute for the creativity and open-ended generation required in unique content creation. By focusing on its strengths—enhancing workflows in predictable programming tasks—it reinforces GPT-4o's role as a powerful productivity tool tailored to specific user needs.

Chapter 6: Limitations and Constraints

While the "Predicted Outputs" feature in GPT-4o offers impressive efficiency gains, it comes with specific restrictions and limitations that users must navigate to fully leverage its capabilities. These limitations primarily affect advanced API functionalities, making it less suitable for tasks that require certain complex features.

One of the primary restrictions involves **function calls**. In many applications, function calls allow the AI to perform dynamic operations, such as triggering specific outputs or integrating with external systems. However, when using "Predicted Outputs," these advanced interactions are unsupported. This limitation means that tasks requiring intricate chaining of operations or API responses cannot fully benefit from the feature. For developers relying on function calls to execute multifaceted workflows, this restriction necessitates alternative strategies for achieving their goals.

Another area where "Predicted Outputs" falls short is in **audio and multimodal generation**. These capabilities, often used for tasks like text-to-speech, image captioning, or multimodal content creation, require a more open-ended approach to AI processing. Since "Predicted Outputs" relies on pre-existing patterns and user-supplied predictions, it cannot effectively handle the complexity and unpredictability inherent in generating audio or multimodal outputs. For instance, creating an audio response from scratch or combining text with visual elements demands a level of flexibility that this feature is not designed to provide.

The feature also imposes restrictions on **max_tokens** and related parameters. Normally, these settings allow users to control the length and depth of the AI's response, tailoring the output to specific needs. However, when using "Predicted Outputs," these parameters are either unsupported or limited in functionality. This means users cannot impose strict token limits or guide the model's output length as effectively as they might in other workflows. For tasks requiring fine-grained control over the response size—such as generating concise summaries or fitting content within predefined character limits—this restriction can be a drawback.

These limitations highlight the trade-offs inherent in the "Predicted Outputs" feature. While it excels in optimizing workflows for predictable and repetitive tasks, it is less suitable for dynamic, creative, or highly customized interactions. For users working with complex APIs, audio and multimodal applications, or tightly controlled output parameters, alternative approaches may be required to meet their specific needs.

Understanding these restrictions is crucial for maximizing the utility of "Predicted Outputs." By aligning the feature with tasks it's best suited for—such as code refactoring, document updates, and data adjustments—users can achieve remarkable efficiency gains while working around its limitations. For more advanced or unconventional applications, however, a broader approach leveraging other GPT-4o capabilities may be necessary to fulfill the task requirements.

The "Predicted Outputs" feature in GPT-4o introduces notable cost-saving opportunities by optimizing token usage, but it also comes with considerations tied to token rejection and billing. Understanding these cost implications is essential for maximizing efficiency while minimizing unnecessary expenses. At the heart of this dynamic is the delicate balance between accurate predictions and the AI's token processing behavior.

When using "Predicted Outputs," tokens from the user-provided prediction are evaluated by the model for compatibility with its internal computations. Tokens that align with the model's intended output are accepted, integrated directly into the response, and processed quickly. These accepted tokens are computationally efficient, reducing the time and resources required to generate the final output.

However, **token rejection** plays a critical role in cost considerations. Rejected tokens—those that do not match the model's output—are discarded but still incur computational charges. For instance, if a prediction includes 100 tokens and 20 of them are rejected, the user is billed for all 100 tokens, including those not used in the final response. This billing strategy underscores the importance of providing precise and accurate predictions, as mismatched or overly broad predictions can lead to unnecessary token charges without corresponding gains in efficiency.

To mitigate costs, users should focus on the **accuracy of their predictions**. The closer the provided prediction is to the intended output, the fewer tokens the model will need to reject and regenerate. For example, when updating a specific property in a codebase, supplying only the stable portions of the code along with clear instructions for the modification ensures that the model processes fewer unnecessary tokens. This precision not only saves time but also reduces token consumption, leading to more cost-effective interactions.

Another way to manage costs is by starting with simpler tasks or smaller predictions. Testing the feature with controlled, predictable inputs helps users refine their approach, improving the accuracy of predictions over time. This iterative learning process minimizes rejected tokens and ensures that subsequent predictions align more closely with the model's capabilities.

It's also important to factor in the overall task complexity. For repetitive or structured tasks, where predictions are inherently more accurate, the cost benefits of "Predicted Outputs" are most apparent. However, for tasks with unpredictable elements or where accurate predictions are difficult to formulate, the risk of token rejection increases, potentially offsetting the feature's efficiency advantages.

In summary, the cost-effectiveness of "Predicted Outputs" hinges on the precision of the user's predictions and the thoughtful application of the feature to tasks where it provides clear advantages. By minimizing token rejection and optimizing the use of accepted tokens, users can achieve significant time and cost savings. This highlights the dual importance of understanding the feature's mechanics and aligning its use with tasks that best leverage its strengths.

Chapter 7: Practical Tips for Using Predicted Outputs

When incorporating the "Predicted Outputs" feature into your workflow, starting small and testing with simple tasks is a practical approach to understanding its potential while minimizing errors. By gradually familiarizing yourself with the feature's mechanics, you can refine your strategies, improve prediction accuracy, and maximize time savings in more complex applications.

Starting Small with Simple Tasks

Simple, repetitive tasks are ideal for initial experimentation with "Predicted Outputs." These tasks allow you to explore how the model interacts with predictions and identify patterns in its processing behavior. For example:

- **Code Refactoring**: Start by updating a single property in a small code snippet. Provide the existing structure as a prediction and specify the desired change. This helps you gauge how well the model integrates your input into the final output.

- **Content Updates**: Test by revising a short paragraph in a document. Supply the unchanged text as a baseline and highlight the specific modifications. Observe how the AI handles the prediction and generates the updated section.

- **Data Adjustments**: Modify a small subset of entries in a spreadsheet or dataset. Include the stable portions as predictions and indicate the fields needing updates.

These controlled tasks provide a low-stakes environment for experimenting with prediction accuracy, token rejection, and overall workflow efficiency. As you gain confidence, you can gradually scale up to more complex tasks.

Strategies for Minimizing Errors

1. **Provide Clear and Concise Predictions**: Ensure that your predictions accurately reflect

the unchanged portions of the task. Avoid including irrelevant or ambiguous information, as this can increase token rejection and lead to unnecessary processing.

2. **Break Down Complex Tasks**: For larger projects, divide the task into smaller, manageable segments. This approach not only reduces the risk of errors but also allows you to fine-tune predictions for each segment, ensuring greater precision.

3. **Use Specific Instructions**: Accompany your predictions with clear directives about the desired changes. For instance, when refactoring code, specify exactly which property, function, or variable needs modification.

4. **Validate Outputs Incrementally**: After receiving the AI's response, review it for accuracy before proceeding to the next step. This iterative validation helps catch errors early, preventing them from compounding in subsequent steps.

Maximizing Time Savings

1. **Leverage Predictable Patterns**: Focus on tasks with consistent structures, such as repetitive coding patterns, standardized content updates, or regular data formatting. These tasks allow the AI to fully utilize the efficiency of "Predicted Outputs."

2. **Optimize Prediction Size**: Strike a balance between providing enough context for the AI to work efficiently and avoiding unnecessary details that may complicate the process. Well-targeted predictions ensure faster and more accurate responses.

3. **Experiment with Streaming Mode**: For tasks requiring real-time feedback, use the streaming feature to receive incremental outputs. This allows you to validate and apply results immediately, reducing downtime between interactions.

4. **Iterate and Refine**: Use early attempts to understand the model's behavior and refine

your predictions over time. Each iteration provides valuable insights into how to align your inputs with the model's strengths.

By starting with simple tasks and adopting these strategies, you can build a solid foundation for effectively using "Predicted Outputs." This step-by-step approach not only minimizes errors but also ensures that you fully realize the time-saving potential of GPT-4o as you transition to more complex and demanding workflows.

Streaming mode offers a powerful way to make workflows more efficient by delivering results in real time, allowing users to interact with outputs as they are generated. This feature is particularly useful for tasks that benefit from incremental processing, where each part of the output can be reviewed and applied immediately. To use streaming mode effectively, it's essential to understand how to integrate it into workflows and avoid common pitfalls when working with predictions.

When using streaming mode, the key is to align its capabilities with tasks that thrive on immediacy and iterative refinement. For instance, in coding, streaming allows developers to see updates line by line as the model processes changes, enabling faster validation and application. Similarly, in content editing, receiving sections of updated text in real time means revisions can be reviewed and adjusted on the fly. This approach not only saves time but also creates a more interactive experience, where users can provide feedback or further instructions without waiting for the entire output to generate.

An effective way to maximize streaming mode is by pairing it with "Predicted Outputs." For example, if you're updating a JavaScript server and adding a new route, the existing structure can be provided as a prediction, and the AI will stream the new additions in chunks. This immediate feedback helps ensure that the changes align with your expectations, reducing the likelihood of errors and unnecessary rework. Additionally, when dealing with large datasets or documents, streaming mode enables you to focus on specific sections as they appear, streamlining workflows that would otherwise feel overwhelming.

However, to make the most of streaming and predictions, it's important to avoid common mistakes. One of the most frequent errors is providing overly broad or inaccurate predictions. When the input doesn't closely match the intended output, the model spends more time rejecting tokens and generating corrections, which can offset the time-saving benefits of predictions. To avoid this, predictions should be concise and precise, offering the AI a clear framework to work with.

Another common mistake is neglecting to test predictions on simpler tasks before applying them to more complex workflows. Starting small helps identify any gaps in understanding or mismatches between the prediction and the expected output. By refining your approach on manageable tasks, you can build confidence and accuracy, reducing errors when scaling up to larger projects.

Overloading the streaming mode with excessive detail or overly complex instructions can also hinder its effectiveness. While the feature is designed to handle real-time interactions, overly complicated predictions may slow down the process or lead to inconsistent results. Striking a balance between providing enough context and avoiding unnecessary detail ensures smoother interactions.

Finally, failing to validate each chunk of the streamed output is a critical oversight. Real-time workflows thrive on quick validation and iterative feedback. By reviewing each section as it's delivered, you can make adjustments immediately, ensuring the final output meets your needs. Skipping this step risks overlooking errors that could disrupt the overall workflow.

By understanding the strengths of streaming mode and being mindful of these potential pitfalls, you can unlock its full potential. It's not just about speed; it's about creating a dynamic and responsive interaction with the AI, allowing you to stay in control of your workflow while maximizing efficiency and accuracy. This balance is what makes streaming mode an invaluable tool for anyone looking to optimize real-time tasks.

Chapter 8: Transforming Industries with GPT-4o

Developers are harnessing the power of "Predicted Outputs" to streamline coding processes, making debugging and refactoring faster and more precise. By allowing the AI to focus on targeted changes within existing codebases, this feature eliminates the inefficiencies of traditional token-by-token generation, offering a smarter, more intuitive approach to handling repetitive or iterative tasks.

One of the standout benefits lies in **faster debugging**. Debugging often involves identifying and fixing specific errors in a codebase without altering the surrounding structure. With "Predicted Outputs," developers can provide the stable portions of the code as a prediction, allowing the AI to focus exclusively on the problematic areas. For example, if a syntax error exists in a JavaScript function, the developer can input the existing code and instruct the AI to correct the error. Instead of reanalyzing or rewriting the entire function, the model adjusts only the faulty line. This targeted correction not only saves time but also minimizes the risk of introducing unintended changes elsewhere in the code.

Refactoring, another critical aspect of development, also benefits significantly from "Predicted Outputs." Refactoring involves restructuring existing code to improve readability, performance, or maintainability without altering its external behavior. Traditionally, this process requires careful manual adjustments to ensure that changes do not disrupt the overall logic. With "Predicted Outputs," developers can supply the current code as a prediction and specify the desired adjustments. For instance, renaming variables, splitting functions into smaller components, or updating a property in a TypeScript class becomes a seamless task. The AI processes the provided prediction, modifies only the necessary parts, and retains the integrity of the untouched sections. This efficiency makes it possible to handle large-scale refactoring projects more confidently and quickly.

Beyond debugging and refactoring, developers are leveraging "Predicted Outputs" to **simplify coding workflows**. Many coding tasks involve repetitive patterns, such as adding new routes in server setups, updating configuration files, or integrating APIs. By using predictions, developers can supply the repetitive portions as a baseline, enabling the AI to generate only the unique elements required for each task. For example, when setting up multiple API endpoints, the developer can input a template of the existing routes and instruct the AI to create a new one. The model integrates the new route while preserving the structure and style of the existing code, ensuring consistency across the project.

The feature also supports iterative development, where small changes are made and tested continuously. Instead of starting from scratch with each iteration, developers can use predictions to carry forward the stable portions of the code. This approach allows the AI to focus on implementing incremental changes, reducing the time spent reworking elements that remain unchanged. Over the course of a project, this can lead to substantial time savings and a smoother development process.

"Predicted Outputs" aligns perfectly with the demands of modern development, where speed, accuracy, and adaptability are paramount. By reducing redundant work, accelerating repetitive tasks, and ensuring precision in targeted updates, this feature empowers developers to focus on higher-level challenges, such as designing innovative solutions and optimizing performance. The result is a more efficient and productive coding experience, transforming how developers approach their workflows in increasingly complex environments.

In content creation, "Predicted Outputs" is a game-changer for making efficient updates to existing articles and blogs. This feature simplifies the process of revising content by focusing on the specific sections requiring modification while leaving the rest untouched. Writers, editors, and content managers can now approach updates with precision, saving time and ensuring consistency across their work.

When updating an article or blog, much of the content often remains unchanged. For example, you might need to add a new section, refine a paragraph, or update facts and figures to reflect current trends. With "Predicted Outputs," you can provide the original text as a prediction and instruct the AI on the specific updates needed. The model processes the unchanged portions of the text as-is and concentrates solely on generating the new or revised segments. This eliminates the need to rewrite entire sections, making the workflow faster and more efficient.

Imagine revisiting an old blog post about a software update. The bulk of the article might still be relevant, but a new version of the software has introduced additional features. By supplying the existing content as a baseline, you can ask the AI to append or modify only the sections that discuss the latest features. This approach ensures that the updated content seamlessly integrates with the original, preserving the tone, style, and structure of the piece.

"Predicted Outputs" also helps maintain consistency when managing multiple articles or posts within a content library. For instance, when applying a brand-wide style change or updating recurring information (like contact details or product specifications), you can use the feature to make targeted adjustments across various documents. The AI processes the shared elements efficiently, focusing on the unique updates for each piece, which reduces the overall workload.

Beyond content creation, "Predicted Outputs" has potential applications in **data science and analytics**, where it can streamline tasks that involve updating and analyzing datasets. Data scientists often work with structured datasets, modifying specific fields or correcting entries without altering the overall format. For example, if a dataset contains outdated product prices, you can supply the stable portions as a prediction and specify which fields need adjustments. The AI evaluates the provided data, updates the necessary values, and retains the structure and integrity of the dataset.

In analytics workflows, this capability is equally valuable for cleaning and preparing data. For instance, when standardizing inconsistent formats (such as date entries or numerical units), "Predicted Outputs" allows the AI to focus on the problematic fields while skipping over correctly formatted data. This selective processing not only saves time but also minimizes the risk of introducing errors.

The feature also supports repetitive reporting tasks, such as generating summaries or updating metrics in periodic reports. By providing a template with recurring elements as a prediction, analysts can ensure that the AI focuses on updating only the new data points. This streamlines the production of consistent, professional-quality reports while reducing the manual effort involved.

Overall, "Predicted Outputs" enhances both content creation and data workflows by enabling targeted, efficient updates. Whether you're revising an article or refining a dataset, this feature allows you to focus on what matters most, empowering you to deliver polished results quickly and accurately. It's a tool designed to not only save time but also elevate the quality and consistency of your work.

Chapter 9: The Future of Predictive AI

The broader implications of predictive AI features like "Predicted Outputs" extend far beyond their immediate applications, signaling a fundamental shift in how humans and machines interact. By enabling AI to work more efficiently within defined constraints, predictive features offer a glimpse into the future of collaborative, context-aware systems that adapt seamlessly to user needs. This evolution isn't just about making tasks faster—it's about redefining the role of AI as an intelligent partner in creative, technical, and analytical workflows.

At its core, "Predicted Outputs" demonstrates the power of user-guided AI. Unlike traditional models that generate responses from scratch, this feature allows users to actively shape the AI's output by providing a baseline. This dynamic interaction paves the way for a more intuitive relationship between humans and AI, where the technology complements human input rather than attempting to replace it. By focusing on precision and efficiency, predictive features allow users to maintain control over their work while leveraging the model's computational capabilities to handle repetitive or time-consuming elements.

The implications for productivity are profound. In industries where speed and accuracy are critical—such as software development, content creation, and data analysis—predictive AI can drastically reduce the time spent on routine tasks. This frees up human effort for more strategic and innovative activities, driving progress in ways that weren't possible before. For instance, a developer no longer needs to manually rewrite unchanged sections of code during a refactor, and a content creator can update multiple articles in a fraction of the time, all while maintaining consistency and quality.

Beyond immediate applications, predictive features like these set the stage for future innovations in AI design and functionality. One potential direction is the development of even more context-aware systems that not only accept user predictions but also learn from them to improve future interactions. By analyzing patterns in user inputs and responses, such systems could anticipate needs more effectively, reducing the cognitive load on users and making workflows even more seamless.

The integration of predictive features into multimodal systems is another exciting frontier. Imagine an AI capable of combining textual predictions with visual, auditory, or spatial elements to create comprehensive, multi-dimensional outputs. For example, in creative industries, a predictive AI might assist in designing multimedia campaigns, blending text updates with layout suggestions or audio enhancements based on user-provided templates. Such capabilities could revolutionize fields ranging from marketing to entertainment, where the ability to produce cohesive, high-quality content across multiple formats is increasingly in demand.

Predictive AI also hints at a future where collaboration between humans and machines becomes more symbiotic. As the technology evolves, we may see tools that allow users to switch fluidly between manual and automated inputs, blending human creativity with machine precision. This could enable entirely new workflows that capitalize on the strengths of both, pushing the boundaries of what individuals and teams can achieve.

Finally, predictive features contribute to the broader goal of making AI more accessible and user-friendly. By simplifying complex tasks and offering clear pathways for interaction, these tools lower the barrier to entry for non-experts. This democratization of AI has far-reaching implications, empowering more people to harness its potential across diverse fields and industries.

In essence, "Predicted Outputs" is more than a productivity tool—it's a step toward a future where AI serves as an adaptable, intelligent collaborator.

By focusing on efficiency, precision, and user-guided interaction, it sets a new standard for what AI can achieve, opening the door to innovations that will continue to shape the way we work, create, and solve problems.

The future of AI workflows is poised to be transformative, driven by advancements in predictive capabilities, real-time processing, and enhanced human-machine collaboration. As AI evolves, workflows are likely to become more seamless, intuitive, and deeply integrated into our daily tasks, pushing the boundaries of productivity and creativity.

One direction AI workflows might head is the development of more **context-aware systems**. These systems will not only understand explicit user inputs but also anticipate needs based on patterns, preferences, and previous interactions. Imagine an AI that recognizes your habits, predicts your next steps, and proactively prepares tools, templates, or suggestions tailored to your specific project. For example, a developer working on a software application could see the AI auto-generate boilerplate code or suggest fixes based on past debugging sessions. This anticipatory behavior would significantly reduce the time spent setting up tasks and allow users to focus on execution.

Another promising area is the **fusion of multimodal capabilities** with predictive workflows. AI systems will increasingly integrate text, visuals, audio, and even tactile feedback into cohesive outputs. In creative fields, this could mean an AI that not only refines written content but also suggests complementary visuals, audio clips, or layouts, enabling fully-fledged multimedia project development within a single workflow. For data scientists, it might mean integrating numerical analysis with dynamic visualizations, where the AI predicts trends and creates interactive charts based on ongoing datasets.

Collaboration between multiple AI systems is another likely advancement. Just as humans collaborate to combine expertise, future workflows may involve interconnected AIs specializing in different domains. For example, one AI could focus on content generation while another optimizes its performance for specific audiences, and a third ensures it aligns with regulatory requirements. These specialized AIs could work in tandem, communicating and adapting to produce outputs that are not only efficient but also highly customized.

The integration of **autonomous decision-making capabilities** into AI workflows is also on the horizon. While current systems require explicit user guidance, future AI tools may act semi-independently, analyzing goals and constraints to propose or implement solutions without constant input. This could revolutionize fields like project management, where AI could independently allocate resources, identify bottlenecks, and suggest actionable strategies to meet deadlines.

As AI becomes more robust, **real-time adaptability** will likely become a defining feature of workflows. This means AI systems that not only process and respond in real time but also adapt dynamically to changes in context. For instance, in a live collaborative environment, AI could adjust outputs as team members provide new feedback or data, ensuring that the workflow stays fluid and responsive.

AI workflows will also likely focus on **ethical and transparent interactions**, addressing concerns about data privacy, algorithmic bias, and decision accountability. Predictive systems of the future could include built-in transparency features, showing users exactly how predictions are generated and providing options for customization to align with ethical guidelines.

Lastly, the **democratization of AI tools** will shape workflows across industries. As interfaces become more user-friendly and accessible, individuals without technical expertise will be able to integrate AI into their processes. This democratization could lead to widespread innovation, as more people bring unique perspectives to the development and application of AI.

In summary, the next phase of AI workflows will emphasize integration, adaptability, and collaboration. These systems will not only handle tasks but actively enhance the way we approach problems, making workflows faster, smarter, and more inclusive. As predictive and multimodal capabilities continue to mature, AI will transition from being a powerful tool to becoming an indispensable partner in shaping the future of work.

Conclusion

"Predicted Outputs" stands as one of the most significant advancements in GPT-4o, fundamentally changing how AI interacts with repetitive and predictable tasks. By allowing users to provide partial predictions, this feature streamlines workflows, saves time, and enhances precision in ways that earlier models could not achieve. Its ability to skip redundant computations and focus only on generating necessary changes makes it an invaluable tool for developers, content creators, data analysts, and professionals across a wide spectrum of industries.

This innovation represents a turning point for AI productivity by shifting the focus from sheer computational power to intelligent optimization. Where earlier models excelled at generating creative and open-ended outputs, GPT-4o adds a new layer of practicality, bridging the gap between human guidance and machine efficiency. It empowers users to take a more active role in shaping AI's responses, fostering collaboration that feels intuitive and results-driven. Tasks that once took minutes are now completed in seconds, not because of faster generation alone but because of smarter interactions.

The implications of "Predicted Outputs" extend far beyond immediate productivity gains. This feature sets the stage for a new era of AI workflows—ones that prioritize adaptability, user control, and real-time responsiveness. It shows how AI can not only handle the heavy lifting of routine operations but also complement human expertise by enhancing accuracy and reducing cognitive load. This evolution is more than just a technical achievement; it redefines what it means to work with AI as a partner.

As AI tools continue to evolve, the impact of innovations like "Predicted Outputs" will be felt in every aspect of work and creativity. Faster, smarter, and more collaborative AI systems will unlock potential previously limited by time and complexity, enabling individuals and teams to push the boundaries of what they can accomplish. This isn't just about saving seconds or streamlining workflows—it's about transforming how we approach challenges and harnessing the full potential of technology to drive progress. With GPT-4o leading the way, the future of AI productivity has never looked more promising.

www.ingramcontent.com/pod-product-compliance
Lightning Source LLC
Chambersburg PA
CBHW070122230526
45472CB00004B/1383